ACKNOWLEDGEMENTS

Several people have assisted me with this pamphlet. Hannah Dee persuaded
me to write it in the first place, and Kate Connelly and Pete Glatter made
very useful comments on the first draft. My greatest debt is to the late
Tony Cliff, who first taught me about the real Lenin, and whose works I have
shamelessly plundered in writing this brief introduction.

ABOUT THE AUTHOR

Ian Birchall, formerly a senior lecturer in French at Middlesex University, is
the author of numerous books and a regular contributor to academic and
political journals. His most recent book is Sartre Against Stalinism. He is a
member of the Socialist Workers Party (www.swp.org.uk)

COVER PHOTOGRAPH
Lenin's mug shot taken after his arrest by the Tsar's secret police

INSIDE FRONT PHOTOGRAPH
Lenin addresses the crowd at the 2nd Congress of the
Third International 1920

INSIDE BACK PHOTOGRAPH
Lenin (at podium, blurred) opening the 2nd Congress June 1920

All photographs from the David King Collection

PUBLISHED BY BOOKMARKS PUBLICATIONS 2005
ISBN 1905192037
DESIGNED BY NOEL DOUGLAS (noel@noeldouglas.net)
PRINTED BY THE BATH PRESS

A Rebel's Guide to

LENIN

IAN BIRCHALL

★1: WHY IS LENIN STILL RELEVANT?

Most historians tell you that Lenin and Leninism are very bad things. Lenin is said to have ruled in a dictatorial fashion over his own party, and later over the state created by the Russian Revolution. He was, we are told, responsible for thousands of deaths and for the creation of a total-itarian society. Stalin merely followed in his footsteps. He is right up there with Hitler and Saddam Hussein as one of the great villains of the modern age. In a recent much-hyped volume, Martin Amis took time out from writing sex and violence novelettes to display his vast knowledge of Russian history, concluding that Lenin and Trotsky "did not just precede Stalin. They created a fully functioning police state for his later use" (Amis, *Koba the Dread*, London, 2002, p248).

People on the left criticise Lenin too, for crushing the workers' rising at Kronstadt, opposing the inde-pendent anarchist movement in Ukraine and destroy-ing the factory committees which sprang up after the revolution.

The real Lenin was a bit more complicated.

Certainly he made mistakes. He could be ruthless — in the interests of the cause, not to line his own pockets — and he fought tirelessly for what he believed to be right. Above all he played a key role in making possible the Russian Revolution of October 1917. The Russian Revolution opened up, all too briefly before it was strangled by Stalin, the possibility of a different world — a world in which production would be for human need and not for profit, a world in which those who worked, not those who owned, would make the decisions, a world in which human beings of all races and nations would cooperate rather than fight, a world in which children would learn about war and poverty in history lessons, astonished that such atrocities could ever have happened.

The world today is very different from the one Lenin knew. Lenin's first leaflets were handwritten — today ideas fly round the globe at the touch of a button. Yet if he came back to life Lenin would recognise some things all too quickly — endless wars, the growing gap between rich and poor, mounting state repression, the pillage of poor countries by rich corporations, the corruption and powerlessness of mainstream politicians. Another world is not only possible but necessary if humanity is to survive. To achieve that, we need organisation. Our enemies are powerfully organised and so must we be.

The central theme of Lenin's life was the need for organisation. What that organisation should look like varied greatly from one time to another — there is no such thing as the mythical "Leninist party". Lenin's work is not a set of recipe books — the best Leninist is not the one who quotes Lenin most frequently. An analysis of Lenin's experience and achievements can help us understand his methods and so make it easier for us to develop the forms of organisation we need for our own struggles.

★2: HOW LENIN BECAME A REVOLUTIONARY

Vladimir Ulyanov, later known as Lenin, was born in 1870, the son of a schools inspector. Russia was then a vast empire where most people lived and died as illiterate peasants condemned to back-breaking work and periodic famine, knowing little beyond their native village unless they were sent off to be slaughtered as soldiers. Serfdom, which in practice made peasants the property of local landlords, was abolished only in 1861. The emperor — known as the Tsar — ruled as he pleased without any parliamentary insti-tutions.

At this time the main left wing force was the Narodniks (Populists). Nowadays they would be called "terrorists". They were mainly students and intellectuals, who believed they had a mission to liberate the oppressed peasants. Their methods often involved throwing bombs, and assassinations. They showed enormous courage but made little impact. Lenin's own brother was involved in such activity and was hanged in 1887.

This turned Lenin into a revolutionary. For a while he

hunted for a strategy to change the world. Eventually he turned to the writings of Karl Marx. Marx argued that capitalism exploited workers, who received far less than the value of the goods they produced. But those exploited workers would become the gravediggers of the system by making a revolution to establish a society based on common ownership. Workers, not peasants, were the key to social change. Peasants who got rid of the landlord could divide the land up among themselves. Workers could not divide up a factory — for them, only a collective solution was possible. Marx insisted that workers would not be liberated by small groups of heroic revolutionaries: "The emancipation of the working class must be the act of the workers themselves."

For Lenin, revolutionaries had to be where the workers were. In the early 1890s there were small study circles of worker intellectuals, determined individuals pursuing knowledge, but remote from their fellow workers. Lenin argued that socialists must involve themselves in real struggles about issues such as wages and working conditions, however limited these might appear to be. In his earliest activity in St Petersburg in the 1890s, Lenin argued that the important job was to train agitators. His own activity involved studying factory conditions and producing leaflets to be circulated in factories.

In 1899 he published his book *The Development of Capitalism in Russia*. It was based on three years research, done in jail and exile. It was full of detail and statistical tables, but the basic point was simple. Russia was still overwhelmingly a peasant country, but modern industry was growing, and with it a working class. The Narodniks were wrong — Russia's future lay with the working class.

This development was double-edged. Men and women were being brutally exploited. But industry was taking them out of the ignorance and isolation of the peasant household, and putting them in factories where collective revolt was possible. There could be no return to a golden age of pre-industrial peasant life: "One has only to picture to oneself the amazing fragmentation of the small producers...to become convinced of the progressiveness of capitalism, which is shattering to the very foundations the ancient forms of economy and life" (*LCW*, 3:382).

In the factory, Lenin argued, workers began to develop socialist consciousness: "Every strike brings thoughts of socialism very forcibly to the worker's mind" (*LCW*, 4:315).

★3:
BOLSHEVISM:
WHAT
IS
TO
BE
DONE?

In 1898 a congress in Minsk with just nine delegates founded the Russian Social Democratic Labour Party (RSDLP). Lenin was not there, having been sent to Siberia for his revolutionary activities.

Under the Tsarist regime socialist activities were illegal or semi-legal. Few revolutionaries enjoyed more than one year at liberty before being arrested and imprisoned in Siberia. Between 1900 and 1905 Lenin was exiled in London, Munich and Geneva.

In 1902 Lenin published *What is to be Done?*, in which he set out his thoughts on organisation. Many of Lenin's critics, and some of his supporters, use this book as a statement of his views on what revolutionary organisation should be at all times and places. This is nonsense. Lenin was writing for one particular set of circumstances. *What is to be Done?* is a historical document rather than a universal recipe. Yet it contains some important arguments that are still relevant today.

A few years earlier Lenin had stressed that trade

union activity pointed workers towards socialism. Now he said the opposite: "Trade unionism means the ideological enslavement of the workers by the bourgeoisie" (*LCW*, 5:384). It was a huge overstatement, but Lenin was making the point that trade unions exist to improve workers' conditions within capitalism, not to get rid of the whole system.

The party's job was to fight for socialism — trade union struggle was a means to that end, not an end in itself. Socialist ideas would not develop automatically. The major socialist thinkers, from Marx and Engels to Lenin himself, had not been workers. Factory workers, often toiling 11 hours a day, scarcely had leisure to read, let alone write. In this context Lenin made the claim, often quoted out of context, that "class political consciousness can be brought to the workers only from without, that is, only from outside the economic struggle, from outside the sphere of relations between workers and employers" (*LCW*, 5:422).

Lenin went on to ask why bourgeois ideas dominated in society. He replied, "For the simple reason that bourgeois ideology is far older in origin than socialist ideology, that it is more developed, and that it has at its disposal immeasurably more means of dissemination" (*LCW*, 5:386). What would he say if he could see the modern mass media?

Workers would not develop "spontaneously" to socialist ideas. The existing order had very powerful means to defend itself. Socialists needed equally powerful means to fight for their alternative.

One vital aspect of this was the establishment of a socialist newspaper. The final section of *What is to be*

Done? called for a newspaper to cover the whole of Russia. For Lenin a newspaper would also be a collective organiser. Such a paper would require a "network of agents", a disciplined and well-organised team of people. Such activity "would strengthen our contacts with the broadest strata of the working masses" (*LCW*, 5:515-516).

Papers like *Iskra* (*Spark*) (on the editorial board of which Lenin served) were printed abroad and smuggled into Russia, or produced clandestinely in illegal print-shops in cellars.

Lenin argued that the party should not be open to anyone who was generally sympathetic to its ideas, but must be an organisation of professional revolutionaries, prepared to devote all their energy to the struggle and to act in a disciplined fashion. As he pointed out, under the repressive conditions existing in Russia, a "broad workers' organisation...supposedly most 'accessible' to the masses" in fact simply made "revolutionaries most accessible to the police" (*LCW*, 5:460).

In *What is to be Done?* Lenin stressed the need for a centralised organisation — "a stable, centralised, militant organisation of revolutionaries" (*LCW*, 5:450).

Only a centralised organisation could deal with the threat from the political police and work around a national newspaper that raised the same issues in all areas. Russian socialism was marked by vigorous debate throughout its history, but once decisions were taken everyone had to put them into practice. Policies could then be tested in practice, and, if necessary, corrected.

This was the principle of what became known as "democratic centralism". There is no great mystery about this idea. It exists in any form of organisation where people get together to achieve something rather than merely discuss.

The next year the RSDLP split. The socialist movement has seen all too many splits, and some people think they prove their Leninism by repeated splits. But here there was an important principle. Lenin wanted a party of people who would work under the discipline of the party and not simply express agreement with it. The final split came over a minor organisational question, but it reflected important differences. Lenin's supporters won the majority and took the name "Bolsheviks" (from the Russian for majority). The defeated side were called Mensheviks (minority). This was only the beginning of the split — many local organisations remained united during the events of 1905. There were various moves to reunite, and the final break only came in 1912.

Lenin's organisational principles helped hold the Bolsheviks together in a difficult period. But soon the course of struggle was to make a completely different kind of organisation necessary.

★4:
1905
PROVISIONAL
GOVERNMENT

In January 1905 a huge demonstration in St Petersburg led by a priest, Father Gapon, was fired on by troops. Hundreds were killed. A new period opened up. The ideas of *What is to be Done?* were forgotten. The job of the party now was to push forward the movement against the Tsarist state. That needed not just a small group of revolutionaries but all the most militant activists in the working class.

In a letter the following month Lenin urged the Bolsheviks to "recruit young people more widely and boldly... This is a time of war. The youth — the students, and still more so the young workers — will decide the issue of the whole struggle."

He stressed that if new people were becoming active, "there is no harm if they do make a mistake" (*LCW*, 8:146).

In September 1905 St Petersburg printers went on strike over piecework pay rates and demanded payment for punctuation marks. The action rapidly spread into a general strike. Striking workplaces sent delegates to a central strike committee known as a soviet (Russian for council) — a new form of organisation. Within weeks this had 562 delegates representing 200,000 workers. It became a political body to defend the interests of the working class. Old prejudices disappeared — although anti-Semitism was widespread, workers elected a young Jew as their main leader. His name was Leon Trotsky.

The previous years of clandestine activity had bred conservative and sectarian habits among Bolshevik activists. It was not easy to adapt to a totally new situation. To begin with many Bolsheviks in St Petersburg were distrustful of the soviets. But in Moscow and elsewhere Bolsheviks played a central role in the soviets. Lenin recognised that the party was in a totally new situation. He immediately travelled to St Petersburg on a false passport.

He argued that the party must be rooted among the revolutionary workers, all those who wanted to fight. For example, Christian workers should be allowed to join the party. Lenin argued that if they wanted to fight but held religious beliefs they were "inconsistent". He believed, "The actual struggle, and work within the ranks, will convince all elements possessing vitality that Marxism is the truth, and will cast aside all those who lack vitality" (*LCW*, 10:23).

One thing separating the Bolsheviks from other political currents was the insistence that workers should be armed. Lenin told how he had been in an argument with some liberals, one of whom said, "Imagine there is a wild beast before us, a lion, and we two are slaves who have been thrown to this lion. Would it be appropriate if we started an argument? Is it not our duty to unite to fight this common enemy?" Lenin responded, "But what if one of the slaves advises securing weapons and attacking the lion, while the other, in the very midst of the struggle, notices a tab reading 'Constitution' suspended from the lion's neck, and starts shouting, 'I am opposed to violence, both from the right and from the left'?" (*LCW*, 10:234).

All revolutions are surprises. The challenge for revolutionaries is not to predict social explosions, but to find ways of responding to new situations. In order to survive long periods when not that much is happening, revolutionary parties need organisation, discipline, routine. But these qualities can become obstacles in a period of rapid change. Before 1905 the Bolsheviks had been a small minority, trying to bring socialist ideas to workers. In 1905 their job description changed radically — now their crucial task was to listen to workers and learn from them in pushing the movement forward. Despite some mistakes, the Bolshevik action in 1905 raised the party profile and membership grew rapidly over the next two years, reaching 40,000. A new generation of militants would play a crucial role in the struggles to come.

★5: HOLDING THE PARTY TOGETHER

The Tsar regained control. Lenin was forced to withdraw to Finland, and then at the end of 1907 moved to Switzerland. There was an enormous loss of confidence among workers. Instead of massive street demonstrations there were tiny groups arguing about the lessons of the experience. Because it had real roots in the working class, the Bolshevik Party was not immune to the demoralisation. In 1907 the Bolsheviks had 40,000 members. By 1910 they were down to a few hundred.

Lenin knew the bad patch would not last — sooner or later capitalism always forces workers into struggle. The job of the party was to hold together and prepare for the next wave. As anyone who follows the Tour de France cycle race knows, there is no point getting to the top of a mountain if you don't know how to come down the other side. The survival of local groups, even if small, meant the party would be able to respond to the upturn when it came.

Lenin was a peculiarly single-minded person. Compared with Marx and Engels, or with Trotsky, he seems very narrow-minded. His writings show little of the broad range of interests in literature, culture and science that they had. Lenin deliberately cut himself off from cultural experience. Gorky recalled that when Lenin heard Beethoven he said that the music was so beautiful it made you want to pat people "when they ought to be beaten on the head" (Lenin and Gorky, *Letters, Reminiscences, Articles*, Moscow, 1973, p289).

He focused obsessively on building the party. Other revolutionaries looked for shortcuts. Gorky was a friend of Lenin's — he had joined the Bolsheviks in 1905, and had written a magnificent account of the revolutionary movement in his novel *The Mother* (1906). In 1909 Gorky organised an educational school attended by just 13 Russian activists. Lenin refused to participate because of philosophical differences with Gorky. When five students and an organiser quarrelled with Gorky and walked out, Lenin immediately invited them to join him in Paris. Every individual was precious.

Some Bolsheviks abandoned the hard slog of party building in favour of cultivating mystical ideas. They talked about "god-building". Lenin attacked these ideas. When there were few members it was important to have clarity about the philosophical basis of Marxism.

There were also tactical arguments. The Tsar had set up a fake parliament called the Duma. It had no real power, and the voting system was rigged so that one landowner's vote was worth the votes of 45 workers. But there were opportunities for workers' candidates to be elected. Some Bolsheviks, including Bogdanov, the author of the splendid science fiction novel *Red Star*, argued that the party should have nothing to do with the Duma. Lenin argued fiercely against this.

The Bolsheviks used the Duma for propaganda and agitation. One of their deputies, Badeyev, wrote, "We used the Duma rostrum to speak to the masses over the heads of the parliamentarians of various shades" (A Y Badeyev, *Bolsheviks in the Tsarist Duma*, London, 1987, p184). Later on the Bolshevik deputies would walk out of the fake parliament to support strikes and join street demonstrations.

★6:
1912:
A
WORKERS'
PAPER

Following big student demonstrations in 1910, the number of strikes rose rapidly in 1911. The working class movement, asleep for several years, began to awake.

The Bolsheviks decided to launch a daily paper. Instead of the small papers which had previously circulated, often devoted to obscure polemics against other socialists, the new paper had to address working people and talk about real problems in their lives. The daily *Pravda* (Russian for "truth") appeared in April 1912 aiming to counter government lies.

It came at just the right time. Earlier that month strikers in the Lena goldfields had been attacked by police, and hundreds were killed or injured. A wave of strikes spread across Russia. For years the Bolsheviks had organised secretively. Those habits, absolutely necessary to protect them from the police, had to be shaken off quickly. Revolutionaries who had become used to swimming against the stream now had to learn to swim with it.

The daily paper was printed inside Russia and sold openly in factories and on the streets. The Tsarist regime could not clamp down completely, but it constantly harassed the new paper. Activists invented all kinds of tricks to fool the authorities. Sometimes the paper was banned and reappeared immediately under a different name — for example, *Northern Truth*.

For Lenin it was vital that the paper should be an organiser. *Pravda* built up a range of worker correspondents, who contributed accounts of their workplace problems and struggles. The paper enabled isolated readers to learn from the experiences of the whole class.

Money was a political question. The paper was financed by its readers. Most workers lived in poverty, but Lenin argued they should be encouraged to contribute at least a kopek (a little small change) every pay day. Lenin would not have turned up his nose at a rich sympathiser, but the regular contributions from workers were more important. They ensured that workers saw *Pravda* as their paper, which would die without their support.

★7:
WAR
AND
ZIMMERWALD

In 1914 war broke out between the major European powers — Britain and France versus Germany, Austria and Russia. This possibility had been widely discussed in the working class movement. In 1910 and 1912 resolutions had been passed at conferences of the Second International (to which all the socialist parties of Europe belonged) committing socialists to act decisively to prevent war.

But in August 1914 it was only in Russia and the Balkans that socialist parties opposed the war. Elsewhere parties and trade unions which had previously taken an anti-war stand now backed the national war effort. In Britain and France socialist leaders joined the government to encourage their fellow workers to go and die in the trenches. Tiny groups of militants opposed the war, risking state repression and the anger of the pro-war public. For those who opposed the war it was a terrible shock to find themselves suddenly totally isolated.

To begin with, Lenin did not believe the reports of the betrayal by the socialist organisations. But soon he was busy trying to pull together the small forces of those opposed to the war.

At the same time he immersed himself in works of philosophy, especially the German philosopher Hegel, who had inspired the young Marx. What Lenin learned from Hegel was that every situation must be seen as an interconnected whole, but that within that whole there were contradictions which made sudden rapid change possible. He described the key features of Hegel's method as, "The leap. The contradiction. The interruption of gradualness" (*LCW*, 38:284). With Lenin philosophy always led back to action.

In September 1915 a small anti-war conference was held in Zimmerwald in Switzerland. All the delegates fitted into four stagecoaches — this was all that was left of the Second International which had represented millions of workers.

Lenin recognised two tasks. The movement required unity, but it also needed clarity. Some at Zimmerwald believed the war could be ended without a revolutionary challenge to capitalism, and that the treacherous Second International could be revived. For Lenin, the only way ahead was to make a complete break with the Second International and smash the old order that had produced the war.

Anxious not to split the unity of the newborn anti-war movement, Lenin voted for the main resolution, which he described as "a step forward towards a real struggle against opportunism" (*LCW*, 21:387). He and five others also issued a statement making clear their reservations about the majority position.

Lenin argued that in Russia workers should see that "the defeat of the Tsarist monarchy...would be the lesser evil" (*LCW*, 21:32-33). For socialists, class was more important than nation — their main aim must be to attack their own ruling class. In the words of Lenin's contemporary, the German anti-war socialist Karl Liebknecht, "The main enemy is at home." But Lenin was unable to convince even the members of his own party of this radical position.

★8:
IMPERIALISM

Throughout the war Lenin continued to argue for clearer understanding. In 1916 he wrote a short book called *Imperialism*, which analysed the causes of war in order to oppose it more effectively.

Marx had already shown that capitalism was based on competition. Every capitalist firm has to strive to outdo its rivals, to produce more cheaply and to sell to a bigger market. But far from being an eternal principle, as the supporters of capitalism claim, competition produces its opposite, monopoly. The most successful firms drive their rivals out of business and take over their assets, or merge with them to form more effective profit-making enterprises. The world becomes dominated by large companies.

In particular Lenin observed the fact that as capitalist firms get bigger they need more raw materials and larger markets to sell in. They cannot exist within national frontiers and push outwards to take over the rest of the world. In the last quarter of the 19th century the imperial powers of Europe colonised most of Africa and imposed their rule on the native civilisations. This was the logic of the system. It wasn't possible to have a more humane capitalism. Lenin wrote, "The capitalists divide the world, not out of any particular malice, but because the degree of concentration which has been reached forces them to adopt this method in order to obtain profits" (*LCW*, 22:253).

Some thinkers in the Second International, like Karl Kautsky, had claimed that as capitalism developed it reduced the tendency to war. That myth is still around today. There are people who claim that globalisation can put an end to war. Lenin argued that the drive to war would continue while capitalism survived. Today capitalism is more multinational than it has ever been. But this doesn't mean that relations between the big powers have become more harmonious. On the contrary, competition and conflict are more intense.

Many things have changed since Lenin's day. Colonialism has largely come to an end. Imperialism can generally exploit Third World countries quite effectively without political rule. But on the essential point, Lenin has been shown to be right. Periods of international cooperation are only interludes.

"Peaceful alliances prepare the ground for wars, and in their turn grow out of wars," he wrote (*LCW*, 22:295). Capitalism still leads to war, as we can see every day on the television news.

★9:
1917:
REVISING
PERSPECTIVES

In January 1917 Lenin addressed a meeting in Zurich, saying, "We of the older generation may not live to see the decisive battles of this coming revolution" (*LCW*, 23:253). He was soon to be surprised.

Russia, with its underdeveloped economy, was suffering greater strain than other nations. In February 1917 women textile workers in Petrograd went on strike, even though the Bolsheviks advised against strike action at this time. Workers were moving ahead of the party.

The strikes spread. A week later the Tsar fled. A Provisional Government was formed, pledged to establish universal suffrage and a constitution. During the strikes workers had revived the organisations invented in 1905, the soviets.

Lenin, still in Switzerland, realised that a new phase of history was beginning. He had not set foot in Russia for almost ten years, but now he was determined to return. He hatched a plan to pretend to be Swedish, although he didn't speak a word of the language. Then the German government agreed to let him travel by train through Germany. In April he arrived back in Petrograd (as Petersburg was now called).

Faced with an unexpected situation, Lenin reconsidered all the fundamental ideas on which he had based his political strategy. Until now he had always argued that Russia was not ready for a socialist revolution. Since there was no parliamentary democracy, he had believed Russia needed a democratic revolution like the Great French Revolution of 1789 (what Marxists referred to as a "bourgeois revolution").

However, Trotsky had argued that Russia could move straight to a socialist revolution. He had developed the theory of "permanent revolution", suggesting a Russian revolution could move straight to workers' power, providing the revolution spread rapidly to other countries. The Bolsheviks regarded Trotsky as a heretic.

Now Lenin came out with a position similar to Trotsky's. He claimed it was possible to move directly to a Bolshevik capture of power in the near future. Members of his own party were shocked — his first job was to win a sharp argument with them.

Lenin also needed a strategy for the peasantry. The working class was tiny compared with the huge peasantry. Widespread peasant revolt began shortly after the February Revolution. Lenin realised that this movement must be linked to the struggle of the workers in the towns. This meant supporting the peasant demand for equal division of the land among those who worked it. The Bolsheviks adopted what had been the programme of the Socialist Revolutionaries (the successors of the Narodniks).

The army, mainly composed of peasants, wanted peace. During 1917 more than 1 million soldiers deserted. The peasants wanted to own their own land. The workers in the towns wanted food. The slogan of the Bolsheviks became "Peace, land and bread".

★10: DUAL POWER

The revolution began spontaneously, but it could not end spontaneously. Some workers were more militant than others. The old ruling class was happy to exploit divisions. The party had to fight for the interests of the class as a whole. As Victor Serge wrote, "The party is the nervous system of the working class, its brain" (V Serge, *Year One of the Russian Revolution*, London, 1992, pp57-58).

Lenin had a double task in this period. He had to relate to the party and encourage it to increase its influence, but at the same time he had to direct his attention to the masses of non-party workers, for without them there would be no revolution. The party had been able to grow because workers remembered its role in earlier struggles. But since the party had real roots in the working class, it was swayed by different trends within the class. Lenin had to judge which to encourage and which to discourage.

Lenin's first job was to get the party in fighting shape. As in 1905, the aim was to draw in all the best militants. The party grew rapidly. At the beginning of the year it had about 4,000 members, by the end perhaps 250,000. In one city, Ivanovo-Voznesensk, membership grew from ten to more than 5,000 in a few months.

The Bolsheviks were not a bureaucratic organisation

in which everyone obeyed orders. In the spring of 1917 the party offices comprised two small rooms and the total staff of the secretariat about half a dozen. Often activity was chaotic — members had to take initiatives rather than wait for orders.

In May Trotsky returned to Russia. Over the previous 15 years Lenin and Trotsky had said some cruel things about each other. But with revolution looming such disputes were irrelevant. Lenin knew when to split — and when to pull together. During the summer Trotsky and his followers joined the Bolsheviks. Trotsky was almost immediately elected to the central committee.

Even the rapidly growing Bolshevik Party needed allies. There was little to be hoped for from the Mensheviks (who believed power should remain in bourgeois hands, and who constantly vacillated as their support declined). But the Socialist Revolutionaries were increasingly divided over their attitude to the Provisional Government, and the left wing moved closer to the Bolsheviks.

The situation was an uneasy balance. Lenin referred to the situation as one of "dual power" (*LCW*, 24:60). No single authority controlled society. The Provisional Government had no intention of challenging the economic power of the capitalists. In the workplaces and localities the soviets effectively ran things. In some factories workers put their managers in wheelbarrows and wheeled them out of the gate to assert their power.

The party had to fight for its ideas in the organisations of the class — within the soviets there were supporters of all the different parties. Lenin stressed the importance of patience in explaining the Bolshevik position — The Bolsheviks must use "comradely persua-sion" and reject the "prevailing orgy of revolutionary phrase-mongering" (*LCW*, 24:63). Only at the end of August did the Bolsheviks win a majority in the Petrograd soviet, one of their strongest areas.

During the summer Lenin and the Bolsheviks faced two severe tests. In July a huge demonstration of work-ers in Petrograd demanded that the soviets should take power immediately. The Bolsheviks argued that this movement must be held back. If the most militant work-ers alone had overthrown the government, they would not have been strong enough to remain in power. More time was necessary before the majority of workers would be ready.

Then a right wing army officer called Kornilov tried to mount a coup to overthrow the Provisional Government and re-establish an authoritarian regime. The Bolsheviks mobilised thousands of workers to defend Petrograd. Railway workers tore up tracks and diverted trains, while other workers fraternised with Kornilov's soldiers. His troops refused to attack Petrograd, and Kornilov was arrested. Lenin made it clear that the Bolsheviks were act-ing against Kornilov, but definitely not in support of the Provisional Government. In fact these events weakened the Provisional Government and strengthened the cred-ibility of the Bolsheviks.

★11:
STATE
AND
REVOLUTION

For Lenin, theory and practice were always linked. Pursuing ideas was pointless unless they led to action. But the most enthusiastic activity was futile unless it was guided by an understanding of how society changed.

In July Lenin had to go into hiding. He took advantage of a few weeks of relative peace to write his most important book, *State and Revolution*. (If you only ever read one book by Lenin, this is the one.) When it was published it caused consternation among many "orthodox" Marxists, yet it was highly regarded by anarchists.

In dealing with the question of the state, Lenin went to the heart of the argument about what socialism is. Opponents of socialism (and all too many of its supporters) have identified socialism with state ownership. Societies have been described as "socialist" just because major parts of the economy were nationalised.

Lenin challenged this view vigorously. He argued that in a society divided into classes the state is "an organ for the oppression of one class by another" (*LCW*, 25:387). It comprises the whole body of repressive institutions used to prevent the inhabitants of a nation from challenging the existing ownership of property and the existing forms of exploitation — the state "consists of special bodies of armed men having prisons, etc, at their command" (*LCW*, 25:389). These institutions are not neutral. The law does not treat rich and poor alike: it is designed to defend the rich and powerful. Lenin was following Marx, who wrote in *The Communist Manifesto*, "The executive of the modern state is but a committee for managing the common affairs of the whole bourgeoisie."

So, Lenin argued, socialists could not take over the state from within, using the existing institutions. He dismissed parliament as a "pigsty", which allows us "to decide once every few years which member of the ruling class is to repress and crush the people through parliament" (*LCW*, 25:422). What distinguishes revolutionaries from reformists, he wrote, is the fact that they believe it is necessary to "smash" the state machine (*LCW*, 25:478). For this, "violent revolution" was required (*LCW*, 25:400).

But what would replace the state? The anarchists thought the existing state could be abolished, and a free, stateless society established immediately. For Lenin this was, unfortunately, impossible. If the working class took over society, the other classes would fight back ruthlessly to regain their privileges. The working class would need a state of its own to resist counter-revolution. Lenin called this the "dictatorship of the proletariat" (*LCW*, 25:402). It would be simpler just to call it "working class power".

Eventually, Lenin argued, society could be reorganised and wealth redistributed. Capitalist waste would be replaced by much more effective production to meet human needs. The old classes would vanish and everyone would be both a worker, doing a job useful to society, and a ruler who participated in a democratic process of deciding how society's resources should be used. The state would become unnecessary and "wither away" (*LCW*, 397-398). Lenin summed up his argument with the words, "So long as the state exists there is no freedom. When there is freedom, there will be no state" (*LCW*, 25:468). Lenin's goal was the same as the anarchists', but he recognised that the path to it would be complex.

Lenin drew on many historical examples, in particular referring to the Paris Commune of 1871, when working people had seized the city and ruled it for ten weeks before being massacred by troops from outside. All members of the workers' government had received the pay of an average worker, and could be recalled at any time by those who had elected them — the same form of democracy as in the soviets. Before 1917 this was the only example of workers taking over society, however briefly, and it was important to learn from it.

State and Revolution was never completed. Lenin had to return to activity. As he noted in the conclusion, "It is more pleasant and useful to go through 'the experience of the revolution' than to write about it" (*LCW*, 25:492).

★12: TIMING THE INSURRECTION

In the summer of 1917 Lenin resisted those who wanted to take power too early. But by the autumn the situation was becoming ripe for such action. It was urgent for the revolutionaries to grasp their opportunities before it was too late. In article after article Lenin argued that there was no time to waste, that it was necessary to prepare the insurrection immediately. By October he was writing to the central committee insisting that "to 'wait' would be a crime" (*LCW*, 26:140).

On the streets there was a mood of expectation: workers were reading Lenin's articles such as "The Crisis has Matured" (*LCW*, 26:74-82). They knew momentous change was imminent, but they needed a centralising force to ensure they all acted together.

Two members of the central committee, Zinoviev and Kamenev, opposed Lenin's plans — and wrote an article criticising him in a non-Bolshevik paper. This could have endangered the whole enterprise. But contrary to the myth that Lenin was a ruthless tyrant, he could not persuade the central committee to expel them from the party.

In Petrograd a military committee was set up by the soviet, and headed by Trotsky. Among its 60 members were 48 Bolsheviks, a few left Socialist Revolutionaries, and four anarchists.

Lenin, who throughout his life had focused on the task of building the party, thought the party itself should call the insurrection. Trotsky, who had greater experience of the soviets than Lenin, had to persuade him that the party's support alone was not broad enough, and that the call should come from the soviets. Lenin was no tyrant — it was his willingness to learn that made him a great leader.

Unlike the Tsar, who sent millions to their death in the war, Lenin did not squander the lives of his supporters. Because the revolutionaries were determined, and showed that they would use whatever force was necessary, the number of casualties in Petrograd was very small. Ten years later the great director Eisenstein made a film of the October Revolution. It is said more people were killed making the movie than died in the insurrection in Petrograd.

Within a day the Provisional Government had collapsed and the Bolsheviks were in power. Elsewhere, notably in Moscow, the resistance was fiercer and there were more casualties. The day after the uprising Lenin declared to the Petrograd soviet, "We must now set about building a proletarian socialist state in Russia" (*LCW*, 26:240).

★13: THE FRUITS OF VICTORY

A new state structure was set up, based on the soviets. Lenin became head of the new government. Though he is often accused of seeking power, he did not want the job. He tried to persuade Trotsky to take it, so that he could concentrate his energies on the party. But Trotsky refused (I Deutscher, *The Prophet Armed*, London, 1970, p325).

The new revolutionary regime immediately began to introduce a programme of radical and far-reaching reforms. One of the first decrees instituted measures of workers' control in the factories.

Private ownership of land was abolished, without compensation. The right to use the land went to those who cultivated it. After a fierce debate a peace treaty was signed with Germany. Russia was out of the war.

Nations which had formerly been oppressed within the Russian Empire were given the chance of independence. Over the next few years five independent states were created, and within the new Russian federation 17 autonomous republics and regions were established.

The old legal code was abolished, and the legal system was completely reformed. Popular courts were set up, with elected judges.

Women gained the right to vote, and full citizenship, equal pay and employment rights. Legal changes began to transform the whole nature of the family. Divorce by mutual agreement was established. As one legislator put it, marriage "must cease to be a cage in which husband and wife live like convicts". Discrimination against illegitimate children was ended. In 1920 Russia became the first country in the world to legalise abortion. Homosexuality was no longer a crime. Such changes put Russia way ahead of the supposedly more advanced nations of Western Europe.

Within a year the number of schools was increased by more than 50 percent, and there were campaigns to teach the illiterate to read and write. University fees were abolished to allow greater access to higher education. Examinations were done away with, and learning based on pure memorising was much reduced. School study was combined with practical manual work, and measures of democratic control were brought in, involving all school workers and pupils aged over 12. Lenin personally gave great attention to the expansion of libraries.

Decrees could only change so much. The task of eradicating ignorance, superstition and reactionary attitudes would take longer. Lenin stressed the importance of the self-emancipation of the working class, saying the revolution must "develop this independent initiative of the workers, and of all the working and exploited people generally, develop it as widely as possible in creative organisational work. At all costs, we must break the old, absurd, savage, despicable and disgusting prejudice that only the so called 'upper classes', only the rich, and those who have gone through the school of the rich, are capable of administering the state and directing the organisational development of socialist society" (*LCW*, 26:409). Despite the terrible hardships of the post-revolutionary period, many working people felt released from the limitations of their old way of life. There are contemporary accounts of workers, after a day in the factory, improvising and producing plays, or attending classes to learn how to write poetry.

Revolutionary Russia saw a ferment of innovation and experiment in literature, painting and cinema. The position of the artist in society was transformed. As the poet Mayakovsky put it, "Streets for paintbrushes we'll use/Our palettes, squares with their wide-open spaces" ("Order of the Day to the Army of the Arts", 1918).

★14: THE FRAGILE WORKERS' STATE

The new society faced many problems. War and Tsarist misrule had left an economy in chaos. The Russian working class was very new. Most workers were the children of peasants who had come to work in the towns. Many were illiterate. The working class was a tiny minority in the midst of a vast peasantry.

Lenin recognised from the outset that there could be no planned economy without the active involvement of the mass of working people. As a newspaper reported his speech, "There was not and could not be a definite plan for the organisation of economic life. Nobody could provide one. But it could be done from below, by the masses, through their experience. Instructions would, of course, be given and ways would be indicated, but it was necessary to begin simultaneously from above and below" (*LCW*, 26:365).

In other words, there could be no "economic planning" separate from workers' democracy. History has shown just how right Lenin was. Whenever planning has been imposed from above, without mass involvement, so called "socialism" has become a grotesque authoritarian travesty.

However, the workers on whom Lenin relied had grown up in a society that warped and stunted their development. As he recognised in 1919, socialism had to be built with "men and women who grew up under capitalism, were depraved and corrupted by capitalism" (*LCW*, 29:69). Russia was less developed, industrially and culturally, than Western Europe, and its economy had been wrecked by the world war. From the very beginning the Bolshevik Party had to some extent to substitute itself for the mass of workers.

There was a great shortage of revolutionary activists with the experience to do administrative jobs. Those who were capable often found themselves doing several jobs at the same time. Victor Serge, a Belgian-born revolutionary who came to Russia to help the revolution, found himself working simultaneously as journalist, teacher, schools inspector, translator, gun-runner and archivist.

This lack of experience was especially serious in the state security machine. The new regime created an organisation called the Cheka (All-Russian Extraordinary Commission to Combat Counter-Revolution and Sabotage). This was undoubtedly necessary. Many of the former privileged wanted to sabotage the new regime. They had to be stopped. But often Cheka employees were people with insufficient commitment to socialist principles who misused their authority. Many innocent people suffered at their hands. It was recognised that this was an emergency measure — in 1922, at the urging of Lenin and others, the Cheka was replaced by a body with more limited powers.

Some revolutionaries expected too much too soon. In 1917 many workers had formed factory committees — Bolsheviks often played a key role in them. But such bodies often represented the interests of a particular group of workers rather than the class as a whole. In March 1918 a report by Shlyapnikov (later leader of the Workers' Opposition) described the chaos produced by workers' control on the railways (T Cliff, *Lenin* vol III, London, 1978, pp119-120). This was contrary to the interests of the workers in general, who needed an efficient transport system. Although committed to workers' control in principle, the Bolsheviks incorporated the factory committees into the trade unions.

If Russia had existed in a sealed bubble, these problems might have been ironed out over a few years. But the great powers of Europe did not want to see the revolution survive. They knew how popular revolutionary Russia was among war-weary workers, and they were terrified that the example might spread.

On the day before the Armistice in 1918 Winston Churchill told the British cabinet it might be necessary to rebuild the German army to fight Bolshevism. Two weeks later he told a meeting, "Civilisation is being completely extinguished over gigantic areas, while Bolsheviks hop and caper like troops of ferocious baboons amid the ruins of cities and the corpses of their victims (M Gilbert, *Winston S Churchill*, vol IV, London, 1975, pp226-227).

Until 1920 a vicious civil war swept across Russian territory. Actually "civil war" is not an accurate description. There were troops in Russia from Britain, France, Canada, the US and 17 other countries, linking up with the various brutal and corrupt Russian leaders ousted by the revolution.

Twice Petrograd nearly fell into the hands of the reactionaries. Lenin discussed the possibility that the Bolsheviks would return to being an underground organisation (V Serge, *Memoirs of a Revolutionary*, London, 1963, p92).

Those who seek to vilify Lenin, such as the authors of *The Black Book of Communism*, produce quotations from Lenin that make him sound like a bloodthirsty brute. In August 1918 Lenin sent a telegram about how to deal with a revolt by kulaks (relatively prosperous peasants, who were enemies of the poorer peasants):

"The kulak uprising in your five districts must be crushed without pity. The interests of the whole revolution demand such actions, for the final struggle with the kulaks has now begun. You must make an example of these people. (1) Hang (I mean hang publicly, so that people see it) at least 100 kulaks, rich bastards and known bloodsuckers. (2) Publish their names. (3) Seize all their grain. (4) Single out the hostages per my instructions in yesterday's telegram" (S Courtois et al, *The Black Book of Communism*, London and Cambridge Mass, 1999, p72).

This looks appalling if the quotation is ripped out of context. There was a vicious war going on, and the counter-revolutionaries were far more brutal than the Bolsheviks. The US commander in Siberia in 1919, General William S Graves, testified that "I am well on the side of safety when I say that the anti-Bolsheviks killed 100 people in Eastern Siberia, to every one killed by the Bolsheviks" (W P and Z K Coates, *Armed Intervention in Russia 1918-1922*, London, 1935, p209). Lenin was no pacifist, and did all he could to ensure Bolshevik victory. The writers of the *Black Book* are not particularly vocal in criticising the violence of George Bush, Tony Blair or Ariel Sharon. It is easier to salve their consciences by denouncing Lenin.

The counter-revolutionary forces were corrupt and anti-Semitic — they had nothing to offer except a return to the discredited old order. Eventually the civil war was won by the enormous determination and courage shown by the Bolsheviks.

Lenin played a crucial role in giving the party political direction. But he was scarcely a tyrant. In the months after the revolution the Bolshevik leadership was often deeply divided on major questions. Lenin was sometimes in a minority and had to argue fiercely to win his position.

Lenin did not consider any task beneath him. He spent much time on very minor administrative details. Compared with modern dictators, his security was very weak. Once his car was attacked by robbers and he was forced to get out while they drove away in it. It took some time before he received any assistance.

He did not seek privilege for himself. In 1918 he issued a "severe reprimand" when the Council of People's Commissars raised his salary (*LCW*, 35:333). There is a letter written by Lenin in 1920, where he very politely asked a librarian if the rules could be bent so that he could borrow some reference works overnight, providing they were returned first thing the next morning (*LCW*, 35:454). It is hard to imagine Stalin or Saddam Hussein showing such respect for library regulations.

★15: THE INTERNATIONAL MOVEMENT

Lenin had always understood that there was no hope for a socialist revolution in Russia unless it fairly rapidly spread to the rest of the world. In December 1917 he wrote, "The socialist revolution that has begun in Russia is, therefore, only the beginning of the world socialist revolution" (*LCW*, 26:386). A workers' Germany, in particular, could have helped Russia economically.

Lenin's hope that the Russian Revolution would spread was realistic. Prospects for revolution in Europe were good at the end of the war. After four years workers were fed up with a system that had caused so much death and destruction. From 1918 to 1920 there were strikes and mutinies, factory occupations, and workers' and soldiers' councils everywhere. Defeated Germany, in particular, seemed on the brink of revolution.

The problem was one of leadership. Almost all the old leaders of the working class movement had supported the war. A new generation of militants had emerged during the war, but they were inexperienced. Nowhere was there a party like the Bolsheviks with experienced leadership and real roots among workers. In January 1919 Rosa Luxemburg, the German socialist, was murdered by her political enemies. Luxemburg was the one leader in Europe who could have argued with Lenin on equal terms.

Lenin argued that there was no point trying to revive the Second International — it was necessary to build a new International. In March 1919 a conference in Moscow proclaimed the Third, Communist, International. Over the next three years three more conferences were held, as more organisations were drawn into the new International.

Before 1914 there had been a deep division in the working class movement, between Marxists on the one hand, and anarchists and syndicalists on the other. After the Russian Revolution many anarchists and syndicalists gave the revolution their support. Lenin was keen to win them over. He spent hours discussing with anarchists such as Emma Goldman from the US and Makhno from Ukraine. In 1920, when European syndicalists had made their way to Moscow, often with great difficulty, some leading Bolsheviks ranted at them about the necessity for the revolutionary party. Lenin adopted a much more positive approach. He argued that the syndicalist idea of an "organised minority" of the most militant workers and the Bolshevik idea of the party were the same thing (*LCW*, 31:235-236). In this strategy Lenin had the support of Trotsky. Many other Bolsheviks took a more sectarian position.

Lenin realised there was a serious problem with what he called "left wing communism". In a period of rising struggle many new militants were drawn into activity. Because they had no memory of defeat, they often underestimated the difficulties of winning over a majority of workers. Many new activists thought that, because they had realised parliamentary democracy was a fraud, all other workers could easily be persuaded of this, and that revolutionaries should refuse to participate in elections. Lenin reminded them that millions of workers still believed in parliament: "We must not regard what is obsolete to us as something obsolete to the masses" (*LCW*, 31:58).

He urged the British Communist Party to seek affiliation to the Labour Party, in order to win over the mass of workers still loyal to Labour, however right wing its leaders were. He insisted that Communists must retain "the freedom necessary to expose and criticise the betrayers of the working class", and concluded that if the Communists were expelled it would be a "great victory" (*LCW*, 31:262–263). What mattered was not an organisational solution, but ensuring that Communist ideas reached the largest possible number of workers.

Some revolutionaries wanted to leave the trade unions altogether because the bureaucrats were corrupt and reactionary. Lenin went so far as to say that revolutionaries threatened with expulsion should "resort to various stratagems, artifices and illegal methods, to evasions and subterfuges", in order to stay in the unions (*LCW*, 31:55). This is often quoted out of context, as if Lenin advocated dishonesty in general. On the contrary, Lenin always argued that revolutionaries should tell the truth to workers. He simply argued that if the union bureaucracy witch-hunted revolutionaries and bent the rules to expel them, then revolutionaries should keep quiet about their party membership in order to stay in the union: "If you want to help the 'masses' and win the sympathy and support of the 'masses', you should not fear difficulties, or pinpricks, chicanery, insults and persecution from the 'leaders'...but must absolutely work wherever the masses are to be found (*LCW*, 31:53).

Lenin could argue vigorously, but he knew how to learn from the movement. The French syndicalist Alfred Rosmer described his first meeting with Lenin, who had written an article calling for an immediate split in the French Socialist Party to form a new Communist Party. Rosmer explained to him it would be much better to wait a few months and win over the majority. Lenin immediately responded, "I must have written something stupid," and changed his article (A Rosmer, *Lenin's Moscow*, London, 1987, p53). Lenin was a leader who knew how to listen and when to change his mind. How different from today's politicians, for whom recognising a mistake is an admission of failure.

In his last speech to the Communist International, late in 1922, Lenin warned of the dangers of imposing the Russian experience on other countries. Revolutionaries everywhere must apply their principles to the concrete circumstances of their actual experience:

"The resolution is too Russian, it reflects Russian experience. That is why it is quite unintelligible to foreigners, and they cannot be content with hanging it in a corner like an icon and praying to it" (*LCW*, 33:431).

★16: RETREAT AND NEP

The German Communist Party, without a stable and experienced leadership, veered from left to right and failed to turn a long social crisis into a successful revolution. Russia remained isolated.

The Bolsheviks won the civil war and retained power, but at a terrible price. The economy was in ruins. The working class itself was in massive decline — by 1921 it was about one third the size it had been in 1917. Many militant workers had left the factories to join the army — a fair number never returned. Others, facing unemployment and starvation, returned to their families in the countryside, where they could get a small amount to eat. The soviets were an empty shell.

The Bolsheviks could not simply hand back power. That would have left the old ruling class free to massacre what was left of working class organisation. They had no alternative but to hang on to power and wait for a revolutionary upturn in the West.

Not surprisingly, there were expressions of discontent in the population. The most serious came in the spring of 1921. Sailors in the naval fortress of Kronstadt, just outside Petrograd, rebelled. Some of them called for a "third revolution". Several of their criticisms were justified. But a "third revolution" was a pure fantasy, and the rebellion threatened the Bolshevik regime. If the Bolsheviks had been ousted, the result would have been not a more democratic society, but the return of the old regime. It was decided to smash the revolt militarily. This was a low point for Bolshevism, but there was no alternative.

Lenin knew that military measures could not solve the real problems. He described the Kronstadt events as "like a flash of lightning which threw more of a glare upon reality than anything else" (*LCW*, 32:279). Again he showed his ability to face an unpredicted reality and adopt the necessary solution. The Russian economy was failing because the party functionaries in charge of various enterprises did not have the ability to run them properly. A suitable balance between town and country had not been achieved.

Lenin introduced what became known as the New Economic Policy (NEP). The requisition of grain from peasants was replaced by a tax which encouraged them to grow more. Some private ownership was restored, and new opportunities for private trade and small-scale manufacture allowed the emergence of a trading class of business people (NEPmen).

The policy staved off economic disaster. Victor Serge recounted, "The New Economic Policy was, in the space of a few months, already giving marvellous results. From one week to the next, the famine and the speculation were diminishing perceptibly" (V Serge, *Memoirs of a Revolutionary*, London, 1963, p147).

This solution shocked many people. Lenin's deep commitment to socialist principles enabled him to advocate such a retreat. He admitted the key test was,

"Can you run the economy as well as the others? The old capitalist can — you cannot." As a result "the capitalists are operating alongside us. They are operating like robbers, they make profit, but they know how to do things" (*LCW*, 33:273).

The NEP was a short-term retreat, not a long-term reconciliation with capitalism. Lenin still hoped a revolution elsewhere would relieve besieged Russia.

★17: LENIN'S LAST STRUGGLE

By 1922 Lenin was very sick. Appalling overwork and the injury from an attempt on his life had left him exhausted. He knew he would not survive to steer the revolution through its most difficult phase.

He was also alarmed at how the revolution was developing. As the working class had shrunk, bureaucracy began to grow inside and outside the party, often adopting methods alien to the principles of working class democracy. There was also a dangerous development of nationalism.

Lenin devoted what strength he had to struggling against the growing bureaucracy. In one of his last articles, "Better Fewer but Better", he recognised that, five years after the revolution, the state apparatus was "deplorable" and "wretched" (*LCW*, 33:487). There could be no quick remedy, only a patient struggle for genuine workers' democracy, with the introduction of more workers into the state machine:

"For this purpose, the best elements that we have in our social system — such as, first, the advanced workers, and, second, the really enlightened elements for whom we can vouch that they will not take the word for the deed, and will not utter a single word that goes against their conscience — should not shrink from admitting any difficulty and should not shrink from any struggle in order to achieve the object they have seriously set themselves" (*LCW*, 33:489).

Lenin's honesty and critical spirit were in stark contrast to the complacency and arrogance that characterised the Russian state under Stalin and his successors.

Lenin was forced to think about who should succeed him. He wrote a short document reviewing the capacities of the other leading Bolsheviks. He was critical of all of them, but singled out Stalin for the sharpest criticism, advocating his removal as secretary-general of the party (*LCW*, 36:594-596).

From the middle of 1922 onwards Lenin suffered a series of strokes. By early 1923 he was unable to intervene in the debates in the party he had built. When he died in 1924 his body was embalmed, transforming him into a sort of saint, something that would have appalled him. His widow, Krupskaya, who had shared his many struggles, urged against this sort of tribute:

"Do not raise memorials to him... To all this he attached so little importance in his life... If you wish to honour the name of Vladimir Ilyich, build creches, kindergartens, houses, schools, libraries, medical centres, hospitals, homes for the disabled, etc, and, most of all, let us put his precepts into practice" (*Pravda,* 30 January 1924).

★18: DID LENIN LEAD TO STALIN?

Many academics, politicians and journalists claim that Lenin's methods and policies led directly to the brutalities and atrocities of the Stalin era. This is a lazy way of explaining history, which fails to examine the complex historical process that led to Stalin. It fits with the idea that history is all about great individuals, that all we need to understand is the psychology of a couple of leaders.

Of course, anything can be proved with selected facts torn out of context. Victor Serge, who joined the Bolsheviks in the middle of the civil war and was later one of Stalin's victims, summed up what was wrong with this approach: "It is often said that 'the germ of all Stalinism was in Bolshevism at its beginning'. Well, I have no objection. Only, Bolshevism also contained many other germs, a mass of other germs, and those who lived through the enthusiasm of the first years of the first victorious socialist revolution ought not to forget it" (*New International*, February 1939).

Lenin's whole strategy was based on the principle that the Russian Revolution would spread to the rest of Europe, then the world. But the revolution failed to spread and, as Lenin understood, it could not be exported.

This isolation was the fundamental cause of what went wrong in Russia. Rosa Luxemburg, often highly critical of Lenin, wrote, "The Russians...will not be able to maintain themselves in this witches' Sabbath...because social democracy in the highly developed West consists of miserable and wretched cowards who will look quietly on and let the Russians bleed to death" (Letter to Luise Kautsky, 24 November 1917).

The real blame lies with those Western leaders like Winston Churchill, who launched armed attacks on the post-revolutionary state, and with working class leaders who defended the Russian Revolution half-heartedly or not at all.

Of course, it is impossible to say what Lenin would have done if he had survived after 1924. But we can be pretty certain what Lenin would not have done.

Stalin's solution, launched when Lenin was safely dead, was "socialism in one country". Instead of encouraging revolutionary movements when they arose anywhere in the world, Stalin positively discouraged them.

The Communist International, in Lenin's day a lively forum where different strategies were debated, became a top-down bureaucratic apparatus in which everyone obeyed the same line. In China in 1927 the Communists were told by Stalin to surrender their independence to Chiang Kai-shek, who used them and then massacred them. In Germany, Communists were told that the Social Democrats were the same as fascists — hence there was no united opposition to Hitler. In the Spanish Civil War, Communists turned their guns against workers who wanted to turn the war into a revolution.

Stalin decided that Russia would have to industrialise on its own. He argued that Russia had to catch up with what the West had done over many years: "We are 50 or 100 years behind the advanced countries. We must make good this lag in ten years. Either we do it or they crush us" (I Deutscher, *Stalin*, London, 1961, p328).

Industrialisation in 19th century Britain was brutal enough. The process was much quicker in Russia and hence the suffering was much greater. What most critics of Stalinism refuse to see is that the system which caused the suffering was essentially the same. Despite state ownership, the economic laws which drove the Russian economy were those of capitalism.

Many of the gains of the revolution were lost. Independent trade unions and the right to strike disappeared, and wages were forced down. Abortion and homosexuality once again became crimes. Artistic innovation was replaced by the drab conservative doctrine of "socialist realism".

Stalin's brutal policy of forcibly collectivising agriculture was the direct opposite of Lenin's position. Lenin had always sought to preserve an alliance with the peasantry.

A new class of bureaucrats, with their own interests, now emerged. The Communist Party, which had consisted of the most dedicated militants (until 1929 party members only earned a skilled worker's wage, whatever their post), now became an organisation of the elite, who looked to Stalin to defend their interests.

Lenin is often accused of introducing the one-party

state. But the Bolsheviks had little choice in the matter. After the successful revolution the Mensheviks and Socialist Revolutionaries proposed a united coalition government if Lenin and Trotsky were excluded, a condition that was clearly unacceptable. The Socialist Revolutionaries then resorted to violence against the new regime — in August 1918 a Socialist Revolutionary attempted to assassinate Lenin.

Lenin was often harsh in arguing with his opponents. But he argued about ideas and policies — he didn't accuse his opponents of crimes they had never committed. In 1921 the Bolshevik Party banned the organisation of factions, but Lenin insisted that "we cannot deprive the party and the members of the central committee of the right to appeal to the party in the event of disagreement on fundamental issues" (*LCW*, 32:261). In the purges and show trials of the 1930s Stalin's victims were accused of fictitious — and often ludicrous — offences, such as collaborating with the Nazis.

There was certainly harsh repression in the civil war period, but it was not comparable to the savagery of Stalin's regime. Victor Serge, who was there and knew what he was talking about, judged that "in theory and practice the prison-state [of Stalin] has nothing in common with the measures of public safety of the commune state in the period of the battles" (V Serge, *Russia Twenty Years After*, New Jersey, 1996, p93).

In order to consolidate his power, Stalin had to kill Lenin's closest associates — Zinoviev, Kamenev, Radek and Bukharin. Stalin's agents hunted Trotsky across the world and murdered him in Mexico. Thousands of rank and file old Bolsheviks were eliminated.

In 1944 Stalin sat down with Winston Churchill, who had helped to organise the invasion of Russia in 1918. Between them they carved Europe up into "spheres of influence" and settled the fate of millions without consultation. Churchill was not stupid. He knew who his real enemies were.

Stalin's most consistent opponents were those who remembered the days of Lenin, and criticised Stalin in terms of the values they had shared with Lenin — above all, Leon Trotsky and his tiny band of followers, but also courageous writers like Victor Serge and Alfred Rosmer. They provided the basis for a genuine socialist movement to re-emerge when Stalinism began to crumble.

★19: LENINISM TODAY

Two things mattered above all for Lenin — unity and clarity. Without the broadest possible unity of working people, action to change the world is impossible. But such action is futile unless it is based on a clear understanding of how society is organised. The two principles may seem at times to contradict each other — hence the turns and apparent inconsistencies in Lenin's writings. Unity without clarity means revolutionaries will be dragged along by the ups and downs of the mass movement, unable to influence it. Clarity without unity leaves revolutionaries splitting hairs among themselves, again unable to influence events.

Much has changed since 1917, and Lenin always reminded us to think for ourselves. But three basic themes which run through Lenin's work remain vital in our day.

Independence of the working class. Our world today is still based on exploitation, and it is only those who are exploited who can be counted on to stand up and fight to change it. We have no illusions that a John Kerry or a Gordon Brown would make any real change. The working class needs its own policies and its own organisations.

We cannot take over the institutions of the state, whether parliament or local councils (though we may use them as a platform). The war on terror, with its use of armed force abroad and attacks on civil liberties at home, shows more clearly than ever that the state machine is a weapon directed against working people. It must be destroyed and replaced.

The other side have enormous resources and are extremely well organised. We need to be organised too. We need centralised organisation, because we face a highly centralised enemy. But it must also be democratic, drawing on the experience of those in struggle. The detailed forms of organisation must be constantly revised in view of the current tasks. But the fundamental necessity for a revolutionary organisation is as urgent today as in 1902.

NOTE ON READING

Lenin's *Collected Works* (Moscow, 1960ff) were published in 46 volumes. I've given references in brackets to quotations, with the abbreviation *LCW*, so that readers can check if they want to. I've added a few other notes on points where people might want to know my source.

In a short pamphlet I have been unable to cover many of the important debates arising from Lenin's life. Anyone who wants to go deeper should consult Tony Cliff, *Lenin* (London, 1985-86, three volumes). This develops the same basic line of argument as this pamphlet. Other useful books are L Trotsky, *The History of the Russian Revolution* (London, 1997), V Serge, "Lenin in 1917" (in *Revolutionary History* 5/3, 1994), A Rosmer, *Lenin's Moscow* (London, 1987), V Serge, *Year One of the Russian Revolution* (London, 1992), M Lewin, *Lenin's Last Struggle* (London, 1967), M Liebman, *Leninism Under Lenin* (London, 1975), M Haynes, *Russia: Class and Power in the Twentieth Century* (London, 2002).

Of Lenin's writings, the most important is *State and Revolution*. Others worth looking at are *Socialism and War*, *The Three Sources and Three Component Parts of Marxism*, "Better Fewer but Better" and *Imperialism*. Many of Lenin's better-known books and pamphlets were published in cheap editions in Moscow before 1991. There are still plenty of secondhand copies around. A very full selection of Lenin's writings, in the process of being extended, is available at http://www.marxists.org/archive/lenin